A blast from the past
I allowed curiosity
better of me!!.

Living Freely, Frankly, and Fearlessly

+ hopefully long into retirement!

lots of love

Tony P.

Copyright © 2024 Rebecca D'Amato

All rights reserved.

This book is sold subject to the condition that it shall not, by way of trade or otherwise, be hired out, lent or resold, or otherwise circulated without the author's/publisher's prior consent in any form of binding or cover other than that in which it is published and without a similar condition including this condition being imposed on the subsequent publisher.

The moral rights of the author have been asserted.

Living Freely, Frankly, and Fearlessly

Rebecca D'Amato

Teacher of emotional education at
The Academy of Emotional Education

Contents

Introduction 1

About Rebecca D'Amato 3

1. The reason you're failing in life is simple 6

2. The role of conflict 10

3. Our need for approval 14

4. We can't fix what isn't broken 18

5. Courage 23

6. Freedom 28

7. Peace 32

8. The consequences of internalised beliefs 38

9. 10 Truths you should know 45

10 Freedom and the fully felt feeling 53

11. Introducing The Panacea Program 61

Afterword 63

Introduction

This book is for all the courageous souls out there who are searching for peace and a more meaningful existence. For too long, you've been dealing with crippling self-doubt and a lack of self-worth. And facing conflict with the people around you when they aren't meeting your needs.

You feel you've tried everything to help yourself: buying into self-healing, reading every book, attending every workshop. But you're now facing the painful realisation that nothing of any real significance has changed and the void inside you still hasn't been filled.

What this book will show you is that you're not broken or in need of healing. The sadness and fear you feel are not illnesses that need to be treated, they're emotions that need to be understood.

The book will give you invaluable insight into the human condition. It will teach you why you are the way you are and show you how to permanently liberate yourself from the advice, opinions, and good intentions of others.

Ultimately, it's an introduction to emotional education and the work I do on The Panacea Program. With emotional education, you'll finally be able to stop all the mind chatter and over-analysis. You'll care much less what other people think and you'll no longer attach your self-worth to status and material things.

About Rebecca D'Amato

My story is textbook. Born, the eldest of three daughters, to wounded and emotionally infantile parents, I grew up in a family home where the dynamic was the wrong way round and had to care for my parents and two younger sisters from a pitifully young age. And, inevitably, emerged into adulthood, a typical people-pleaser. A doormat who was desperate for the approval of everyone I met.

My journey to courage, freedom and peace began in the winter of 2001. It got off to a good start using person-centred therapy, but then, sadly, I fell down the New-Age rabbit hole, where I learned to outsource my dreams and give what little power I possessed away to all manner of other-worldly beings. This simultaneously reinforced my adolescent programming, which dictated my emotions needed to be other, different, better, to what I was really feeling.

For many years, I rented temporary relief from frequent bouts of depression and suicidal ideation.

But, eventually, I began to understand that I wasn't broken, ill or in need of fixing. I'd simply been emotionally stunted from a young age. And now I was a frightened thirty-something child, trying to navigate the world without a compass.

My journey was lengthy, expensive, and unnecessarily complex. But I'm grateful for it all, because it's enabled me to create The Panacea Program: a learning experience that's the exact opposite of what I went through myself.

If you're tired of sugar-coated fluff and you're ready to accept that there are no quick fixes, then I hope you'll join me on The Panacea Program.

1.

The reason you're failing in life is simple

"The number one reason people fail in life is because they listen to their friends, family and neighbours."

~ Napoleon Hill, American author.

When our lives are an overwhelming mess, and we believe that our many issues are insurmountable, what we most need is simplicity.

"I despise my job."

— So change it!

"My romantic relationship isn't working and it's making me miserable."

— So end it!

"Some of my friends are often hurtful and my

relationship with all of them feels one-sided."

— So get rid of them!

But all of this is easier said than done.

If you're already exhausted and have a mortgage and/or a family to provide for, changing your job feels like a risk.

If you end your romantic relationship, you fear judgement and criticism from those who believe your other half is 'such a nice person'.

And if you dump all your friends at once, you fear feeling lonelier than you already do. And that's a risk too scary to even contemplate.

We complicate things for ourselves

In our efforts to cope with what's making us miserable, we avoid the simplest solutions and do the opposite. Making our lives and situations much more complicated than they really need to be.

For example, we might spend years, or even decades, in therapy. We might practice New-Age beliefs or collect self-help books that we'll rarely finish. And all the while we're convincing ourselves we're 'doing something ' to help ourselves.

And you *are* doing something. As opposed to all the people in your life who should be doing something, but aren't.

You're showing up in therapy rooms, retreats, and workshops too numerous to mention. But at the end of it all, you must face the painful realisation that nothing of any real significance has changed.

It's hardly surprising that this happens. Because most of us aren't aware of what's at the root of our unhappiness.

The truth about why we're unhappy

None of us arrives at our first therapy session and says:

"I'm here because I spend my entire life pleasing others so they won't disapprove of me."

Or

"I spend my entire life trying to win the love and approval of other people. But I don't even like 99% of them and I'm quite sure they don't like me either."

And this isn't because we can't admit the truth. It's because we don't know what the truth is.

Our actions are largely unconscious. We're not aware of how much we long to be perceived in a good light by the people around us. Or how much we've been programmed to believe we should say yes to anything and everything just to keep them happy.

We've been conditioned from birth to believe our happiness lies in the hands of other people. If we please them, they'll show they like, love and approve of us. And that gives us the affirmation we need that we're okay people and we're living our lives well.

But it's our relationships with others that are our greatest source of emotional pain.

Often we believe that our biggest sources of emotional pain are unresolved issues from childhood and anything related to our finances. And while these two problems do contribute to our misery, they are not the cause of it *or* the solution.

2.

The role of conflict

"Whenever you're in conflict with someone, there is one factor that can make the difference between damaging your relationship and deepening it. That factor is education."

~ William James, American philosopher and psychologist.

We've been conditioned to accept conflict as the norm in every type of relationship we have. It's in our relationships with our parents, children, significant others, friends and work colleagues.

This conflict shows up in the form of:

- The ever-present elephant in the room
- The endless whataboutery we endure

from others
- Those who repeatedly bring up shit from years ago
- The tantrum throwers
- The perpetual victims
- The blamers.

Not forgetting the most significant of all: those who refuse to listen.

I could add more, but I'm sure you get the picture.

For all their faults, we love many of these people — so much so that life without them is unthinkable. Even though these people are often the ones we want to banjo with the frying pan!

Then there are those we could easily live without. Yet we continue to put up with them and their behaviour at the expense of our own peace. None of us needs an expert to tell us we shouldn't be doing this. But the fact we do shows how afraid we are of causing them unhappiness.

What all these people have in common is that they drain us — literally. As the universal life-force flowing through us stops flowing, the outcome is overwhelming exhaustion.

We can try to counter that by booking a break,

having a nap or changing our diets. But it's soulful exhaustion rather than physical — and no amount of sleep, lettuce or expensive multivitamins will alleviate it.

When these methods don't work, we turn to talking therapies, alternative medicine, self-help books, and New-Age beliefs. And we're quick to diagnose ourselves with depression and buy into the belief that we're broken and need to be fixed.

Many of our relationships are, sadly, a case of 'any port in a storm' because we're afraid of being alone. It never occurs to us to ponder whether or not we're worthy of being treated better.

Deep down we carry a great deal of hurt in our hearts, wishing our relationships could be more reciprocal, empathetic, and supportive. And wishing people would listen more and be kinder.

We're convinced we *need* the people we love. We make endless excuses for their behaviour and simultaneously remind ourselves of their many wonderful characteristics. This prevents us from doing the unthinkable and expelling them from our lives.

But that's often what we really need. At least

until they can learn to communicate without using personal insults or whataboutery. Or until we become so emotionally intelligent, we can learn to live with them at arm's length and on our own terms.

3.

Our need for approval

"A truly strong person does not need the approval of others any more than a lion needs the approval of sheep."

~ Vernon Howard, US Author.

We endure unacceptable behaviour from others because we're programmed from an early age to believe our happiness depends on their approval. And if we do all we can to ensure they like/love us, our lives will be rosy.

In my former profession as a transpersonal psychotherapist, we referred to 'okay 'and 'not okay 'signals to describe our need for approval.

An 'okay 'signal is one that shows the other person likes and accepts us. It could be anything, from giving us a smile or hug to buying us a gift. But, above all, it's their willingness to keep showing up in our lives.

By contrast, a 'not okay' signal could be anything from a disapproving look, tut or sigh to criticism, threats and verbal abuse.

We find ourselves constantly striving for 'okay' signals to the point where it becomes exhausting. And if we get a 'not okay' signal it triggers unwelcome emotions. We start to worry we've upset the other person — and what they might be thinking about us, if we have. This can last for days, or even weeks, as our anxiety increases.

You may believe it's not possible to be emotionally honest and authentic with the people in your life. Maybe you're sick and tired of their tantrums or their refusal to own their part in the problem. Maybe you fear they'll become threatening or abusive if you try to bring up your issues.

Either way, you know, if you try to be the peacemaker, it will just stir up more conflict — no matter how carefully you choose your words.

What you're really afraid of

Contrary to what you might believe, you're **not** afraid of how these people will react if you try to talk about your issues.

What you're really afraid of are the feelings you felt throughout your childhood. When your feelings weren't acknowledged or considered. Or, worse, when you felt invalidated, humiliated or chastised.

Because those feelings hurt — they hurt *a lot*.

The cycle of emotional illiteracy

The familial cycle of emotional illiteracy runs from one generation to the next. Regardless of financial status, race, religion or class. Ninety-eight percent of us are raised to compartmentalise our emotions — whether they're good, bad, right, wrong, acceptable, unacceptable, welcomed or feared.

More significantly, when we were young and expressed our emotions in a way that was inconvenient to our parents or primary caregivers, it hurt. This hurt was made worse because those who caused it were the people we depended on to love and protect us.

The problem is that the cycle of emotional

illiteracy continues. And, as a result, emotional safety simply isn't a thing. It's not even considered, let alone discussed.

How emotional illiteracy leads to conflict

Emotions make up a huge part of what and who we are as humans, yet we know very little about them. A consequence of this lack of knowledge is an absence of emotional honesty, communication, and understanding. Without these key things, conflict, both inner and outer, is the inevitable outcome.

In adulthood, we find ourselves coping with unresolved emotional pain and trying to avoid further emotional wounding. But this is keeping us in a perpetual cycle of utter exhaustion, which the self-appointed gurus will tell us is depression and/or low self-worth.

The truth is, there's nothing wrong with your self-worth, thank you very much. And depression is nothing more than your soul trying to tell you it's tired of playing the part of the person you were forced to become.

4.

We can't fix what isn't broken

"The New-Age movement has become middle-aged, and quite frankly it needs retiring, people are exhausted with the journey"

~ Caroline Myss, American author.

When you start trying to 'fix 'yourself — whichever route you take — you'll learn a new set of fashionable buzzwords and expressions, like:

"I need to work on myself."

But working your yourself is actually the barrier to happiness. We're human beings, not human doings. Real, tangible and lasting growth will only begin when you accept your feelings are perfectly natural and learn to be comfortable with them.

"If I peel back another layer of the onion..."

There is no onion. The onion has proved a magic money-spinner over the last 40-years. It gives us a free pass to avoid what we know we must do, but are too afraid to do — and oils the wheels of the £70-billion-a-year self-help industry. But there are no layers and there is no complexity, there's simply an absence of knowledge.

"I need to process this."

What the fuck does that even mean?

This was my own go-to expression during my two-decade-long trip on the not-so-healing merry-go-round. Consequently, I learned to live in my mind rather than my soul.

I'd be analysing and over-thinking in an attempt to come up with answers to my misery. And, at the same time, I'd be talking about the same problems repeatedly to my friends and therapist.

Saying we need to process is a meaningless expression that hands us another free pass to avoid confronting what scares us.

You don't need to 'fix 'yourself

When we seek help, we're labouring under the misapprehension there's something wrong with us. That we need to be healed or 'fixed'.

But you can't possibly solve a problem if you're not aware of what the problem is to begin with.

This is why we're Googling for help with things like:

- Self-esteem
- Childhood trauma
- Assertiveness
- Self-confidence.

But the truth is, these things aren't the cause of your unhappiness — they're just the symptoms.

You need an emotional education

The real cause is the emotional education you didn't receive in childhood. And the absence of **Courage**, **Freedom,** and **Peace**. But you're never going to type *those* three words into Google, because you don't know it's those things you need.

It's not possible to find Courage, Freedom,

and Peace when you're raised in a climate of emotional and soulful illiteracy — which, sadly, 98% of us are.

We emerge into adulthood, afraid of, and demonising, our own emotions. And we go to extraordinary lengths to avoid emotions, like sadness, that make us uncomfortable. Especially because deep sadness can so quickly be labelled as depression.

But when we're pretending to feel the emotions we should welcome — like joy, happiness, and optimism — we give an Oscar-worthy performance. These are the emotions that keep us and everyone else comfortable at the expense of our own happiness and success.

A life without emotional and soulful education is merely an existence. We don't know how to respond to our emotions, or the emotions of others, in a loving, supportive or balanced way. Instead, we often make guesses and assumptions. We blame ourselves and those we care about for not meeting our needs.

Things get even more confusing when we realise the needs we're struggling to fulfil, from within ourselves and from external expectations, aren't even our own. They're the needs of someone we were taught we should be rather than the person we really are.

You'll be surprised and delighted to learn how little you know about yourself beyond the superficial. The real, authentic, unique you was lulled into a deep sleep a long time ago, by parents who raised you with the only resources they had available.

In most cases, they had your best interests at heart. But the essence of you never died — and that's how you know you're destined for better than the deal life has dealt you.

It's how you know you have something magnificent to share with the world. And, above all else, it's how you know that having zero fucks left to give about what other people think is the recipe for a happy and successful life.

5.

Courage

Internalised belief: 'I'm untrustworthy'

"Courage is resistance to fear, mastery of fear, not absence of fear."

~ Mark Twain, American writer and humorist.

When we're deeply unhappy in many different aspects of our lives, we're aware we need to make changes. But those changes take courage that we simply don't have.

Why you lack courage

Here's a simple explanation that will help you understand why that courage is lacking.

Imagine you're 18 months old, sitting on the living room floor, when suddenly you see a spider. It's huge and hairy and you can clearly see its eyes. And it's hurtling towards you at what seems like a thousand miles an hour.

You've never seen a spider before, so your self-preservation instinct is on high alert for potential danger.

You begin to cry and point at the spider, while backing away. But your parent or caregiver responds with, "Oh, for fuck's sake, shut up! It's just a spider!"

In that moment, you learn that:

- Your emotions aren't valid
- Your distress doesn't matter
- You should ignore your natural instincts
- You can't trust yourself to know when you're afraid.

When you're taught that you can't trust your own feelings, the message you internalise as a child is, 'I can't be trusted. 'And this is reinforced every time your parents respond to your concerns in the same dismissive way.

When you've internalised the belief that, 'I'm untrustworthy', it follows that you lack courage.

You feel you can't rely on yourself

In childhood, the approval of our parents is the single most important thing in our lives. Anything that feels like it may threaten our place in the family unit is too terrifying to contemplate.

By the time we're two years old, we're already contorted out of shape. The unique, individual soul we were at birth is lost as we learn to adapt and adjust our true essence to stay emotionally safe.

When you learn not to listen to yourself, you're left powerless. In adulthood, this manifests as an over-reliance on experts and other people for answers, guidance and advice.

You're stuck in a perpetual cycle of conflict

As a psychotherapist, I'd meet clients in their forties and fifties. They'd tell me it still hurt when others ridiculed their fear of spiders. And, though they'd laugh along, they really wanted to yell, "I don't like them, okay?! I hate them, they send a chill down my spine." But they never dared to say it because they didn't understand they had the right to take ownership of their fear.

If you can't admonish a bunch of piss-taking friends for laughing at your fear of spiders, it's no wonder you can't find the courage to:

- Put your own wants and needs before those of others
- Ditch the reliable salary and branch out into self-employment — doing something that makes your heart sing
- Tell someone they've hurt you
- Disagree, when you know the outcome will range from disapproval to a mouthful of personal abuse
- Say no to a favour when you're exhausted to the point of emotional and physical collapse.

A lack of courage keeps you stuck in a perpetual cycle of conflict, where you feel disempowered and are constantly seeking approval from others. But you can't do anything about that if you're not aware that a lack of courage is the problem.

The £70-billion-a-year self-help industry is stuffed to the gills with people queuing up to sugar coat the issue. They'll say you have low self-esteem, but this isn't true.

The real problem is that you're surrounded by

people, circumstances, and events you feel you don't have the courage to change.

6.

Freedom

Internalised belief: 'I'm unacceptable'

"Between stimulus and response there is a space. In that space is our power to choose our response. In our response lies our growth and our freedom."

~ Viktor E. Frankl, author of Man's Search for Meaning.

When we're struggling and looking for help, it's unlikely we'd type the word 'freedom' into Google. After all, we live in the affluent West. We have a democratic right to vote, and a right to express our individuality in terms of religion, dress, and sexuality. So why would we think we don't have freedom?

In truth, you don't have freedom where it really counts.

- Like the freedom to:
- Express yourself with emotional honesty
- Share your true opinions
- Talk about what **you** want and need — unless you're talking to a therapist
- Say no to people
- Establish firm boundaries and stick to them.

We're raised to play it safe, to follow the herd, and develop a hive mind. To not rock the boat or dare to be different. And to ridicule those who are different or label them as troublemakers.

You don't feel free to be yourself

The name of the prison we're not aware we're living in is 'HMP Unacceptable'. We're imprisoned by familial norms, societal conditioning, and conformism. And it's the belief that we're unacceptable beings that prevents us from breaking free.

Here's a simple example to illustrate why we're not actually free.

When we're children, we display perfectly natural emotions. But our parents are sometimes unwilling or unable to respond to those emotions in a healthy manner — and they admonish us instead.

But, as children, we don't have the life experience or intellectual capacity to understand it was the *emotion* that was unacceptable. So we internalise the negative response from adults to mean, 'I am an unacceptable person'.

You put others' feelings before your own

From that point on, we spend our lives striving to be acceptable to others and tying ourselves up in knots in the process. We'll wear ten masks before lunchtime, trying to be ten different people to ten different people. The thought of being authentic in manner, character, opinions, and expression is unthinkable, because we fear it will cause someone else distress.

We also hide our talents, skills, and abilities, in case we upset an underachiever in our family or circle of friends.

The consequence of that is often financial

struggle or an unfulfilling work life. But the internalised fear of being perceived as unacceptable takes priority over everything else in our lives.

What we need to understand is that the feelings of others are not our responsibility.

7.

Peace

Internalised belief: 'I don't matter'

"Peace is not the highest goal in life. It's the most fundamental requirement."

~ Sadhguru, guru.

If you could make a list of all the things you wish you could have and how you'd like your life to be, I imagine it would look something like this:

- A loving and supportive partner/soulmate
- Friends — minus the elephant in the room
- Financial security

- More free time
- A deeper connection with people — especially your family.

But something is missing from that list. Something it probably wouldn't have occurred to you to include. And that something is peace.

Conflict is accepted as the norm

Conflict is the inevitable outcome of our daily interactions with the people around us. And we rarely, if ever, stop to ponder peace.

The word 'peace 'only enters our consciousness when we're totally burned out. Maybe, in the quiet interlude following a heated row, we might place our head in our hands and whisper, "I just want some peace."

But that's as much consideration as we give to our need for peace and how vital it is to our wellbeing.

Is this because we perceive doing so as pointless? Do we believe, even if we're not aware of it, that peace is unattainable?

We end up with such a mindset because three very significant words are missing from our vocabulary when we're growing up. Those three words are, 'Self, I, and Me'.

You disregard yourself to keep others happy

Self, I, and Me don't factor in our lives. Instead, we're programmed from the youngest age to believe our purpose in life is to keep others happy. And if we do that, we'll get the aforementioned 'okay 'signals from them in return.

These 'okay 'signals become our every reason for living and breathing. And without them, we feel worthless, useless, aimless, and despairing.

Sadly, in adulthood, many relationships — whether they're familial, romantic, or friendships — become a case of 'any port in a storm'. We endure the most unacceptable behaviour from others in exchange for those signals that tell us we are okay people.

Believing we're okay without these people takes a level of courage that nobody ever instilled in us.

Instead, we're taught to think we're selfish for considering our own wants and needs — and that to be selfish in this regard is unthinkable.

We must ensure that others are kept emotionally comfortable at all times. This means any thoughts we might have about making changes for our own fulfilment aren't an option.

If we dare to make those changes, we know the 'not okay 'signals will come thick and fast and we don't want that — it hurts.

Emotional pain is part of life

Emotional pain is something we were never taught how to deal with. We were only ever programmed to avoid it, at all costs.

But the bitter truth is that there's no avoiding emotional pain, because it's going to happen anyway. Sadly, we all experience loss, disappointment, grief and financial struggles.

The other point is that we don't start out at the point of despair. We start with sorrow, driven by the fear of what other people think. It only morphs into despair when we don't have the emotional education to respond to that initial sorrow in a healthy way.

Emotional pain is an inherent part of life — in the same way as sadness and fear. None of these issues are illnesses that need to be healed, they are emotions that need to be understood.

Until that understanding is reached, conflict, both inner and outer, will remain a daily headache in our lives. This is often accompanied by an even greater headache, caused by attempting to avoid the conflict we know is coming.

Rather than face that conflict, we exhaust ourselves by pleasing, appeasing, and saying yes to things we want to say no to.

The exhaustion you feel is soulful

This level of exhaustion we experience isn't physical — it's soulful. Because the lack of inner peace is even greater than the outer peace that involves others.

When we think of the word 'exhaustion', we automatically think about sleep, resting, a change of scene or a break from routine. But when exhaustion is soulful, no amount of rest or trips to new places will relieve it.

Deep down, we know what's hurting, why it's hurting and precisely what we need to do to make it stop. None of us, regardless of our intellectual intelligence (IQ) and emotional intelligence (EQ), needs an expert to tell us what we need to do, we already know. We simply lack the courage and freedom to do it, and that means, sadly, we'll never experience peace.

You feel you don't matter

Earlier in this book, we explored the origins of two of our internalised beliefs: 'I am untrustworthy', and 'I am unacceptable'.

But there's a third belief that we internalise in childhood, when our emotions are dismissed, ignored or derided. And that belief is, 'I don't matter'.

When our emotions were invalidated in childhood, and often resulted in some form of punishment, we rationalise the belief, 'I don't matter', because our emotion(s) didn't matter. But what we didn't have the wherewithal to understand is that it was the emotion that didn't matter, *not* the Self, I or Me.

8.

The consequences of internalised beliefs

"It's not a question of learning much, it's a question of unlearning much."

~ Osho, Indian philosopher.

To recap, by the time you reach adulthood — and whether you're aware of it or not — you've internalised three beliefs. These beliefs are that you're untrustworthy, you're unacceptable as a person and you don't matter.

Then, just when you think it can't possibly get any worse, you learn that you're shameful, too. Because shame is the emotion we experience when we understand we have upset our parents for emoting in a normal, natural, and inevitable fashion.

We want to feel like we matter

The outcome is a poor self-concept. The belief that Self, I, Me doesn't amount to a hill of beans, but we still *want* to matter.

We become desperate to prove our value, to prove we're not shameful, and to prove we *do* matter. Because feeling like we don't creates an aching void, a feeling of something missing, a gnawing emptiness and a yearning for acceptance.

At around the age of eight or nine, we learn two things that are quite remarkable and that set the stage for the furtherance of our suffering. The first is that status makes the pain go away. The second is that 'material stuff 'means we matter because it shows we're 'someone', we've 'made it 'in life, and we're successful.

It's intoxicating and addictive — until it isn't.

We crave what our true nature desires

One day, about 12-years ago, I was scrolling on Facebook, when one post caught my eye. The post had 1.6 million comments, and over 10 million 'likes'.

 The post had no words, it was simply a picture

of a magnificent treehouse.

The treehouse had numerous beautifully furnished rooms and was situated in a forest that was so lush I imagined I could smell the foliage, trees, and abundant flowers.

In the near distance, through the surrounding trees, was a beach with the cleanest sand and the clearest water lapping at the shore.

I was instantly intrigued, because I'd never seen a post with so many comments or likes before. So I began to read what people had posted under the image.

You might be thinking there was nothing unusual in this, but I was still reading two hours later. Even when it became apparent that all of the 1.6 million comments said a variation of the same thing, which was 'if only'.

I don't know why I remained transfixed or why I couldn't tear myself away from repeatedly reading the words, 'if only'.

Eventually, when I did stop reading, I sat for what seemed like an age, because something was niggling me. I was already aware that all the 'if onlys' were because the people typing these words were living perpetually exhausting lives, but there was something else. Another, deeper reason why they each felt that an existence in a treehouse by a beach was so deliciously appealing.

I decided to sleep on it. But before I nodded off, I asked Soul/creator/universe/God to solve the niggle.

The next morning, although I'd forgotten all about the treehouse, Soul suddenly said, 'it's other people.'

I got it immediately, what those 1.6 million people wanted was solitude. In that moment of staring at that glorious photo, they'd entered their soul space. And in that beautiful moment, they'd become aware that they didn't need people.

We're convinced we need the people in our lives because we're shameful, unacceptable, and untrustworthy individuals. And we need constant validation, acceptance, praise and compliments to function. But the truth is, we don't **need** other people. We love them, so we **want** them in our lives — but want and need are two very different things. Soul is aware that we are more than capable of providing ourselves with the all the validation, acceptance, praise, and compliments we can handle.

Your soul is emotionally intelligent

We live super-busy lives. We endure daily conflict, unhealthy relationships and unfulfilling jobs. The unsolicited opinions, advice, and good intentions of other people. And fear porn on our 24-hour news channels

To top it off, we drag around the weight of our internalised beliefs: 'I'm unacceptable', 'I'm shameful', 'I can't be trusted', and 'I don't matter'.

The familial emotional illiteracy that runs from one generation to the next, is just as soulfully illiterate as is it emotionally illiterate. Therefore, the word 'soul 'is never mentioned. If it is, we're taught to equate it with religious connotations or the mad cat woman with the crystal ball who lives down the street.

Meanwhile the egregious New-Age movement has hijacked spirituality for profit, encouraging us to believe that metaphysics is spirituality when nothing could be further from the truth.

That's why I prefer to use the word 'soultuality'. Because the soul is our storage space for the wisdom we were all born with but don't yet trust. It's our capacity to love and be loved in the true meaning of the word.

It's also our ability to heal ourselves of physical disease (dis-ease). Because physical illness is often a manifestation of unresolved emotional pain.

Soul is the reason why we know what we know — even when we don't know how or why we know. But we pretend we don't know because it makes life easier. That is, until it doesn't and we can no longer ignore it.

Among the many things we know is that we have a true nature underneath all the false internalised messaging. A core, or essence that's unique to us and longs for freedom in every form.

We know we'd be happier living in a treehouse, in a lush forest by the seashore. Not just because of the utter exhaustion of conflict, but also because living close to, and communing in, nature is our natural state of being.

We need less stuff and more meaning

We weren't put here on Earth to do the daily commute. Or to sit in windowless offices, doing jobs that insult our unexplored intelligence and further offend our yet-to-be-known-and-trusted wisdom.

We know we want less 'stuff 'and more meaning in every aspect of our lives.

On a daily basis, we're doing this dance with life, pretending not to know what we know, so we remain safe from criticism, judgment, and emotional hurt. And to preserve our status and accumulation of material possessions that, up to now, have gone some way to filling the void.

But, in truth, only knowledge fills the void. And the heartbreaking thing is, the knowledge is all so damned simple. It's not lengthy or complex. There's nothing that need cost money. Nothing to memorise, visualise or find time to accommodate in your busy schedule.

It's all simple. The type of stuff we'd have learned if we'd all grown up in an ideal world, with emotionally mature parents who'd raised emotionally well-adjusted children.

9.

10 Truths you should know

"Children are not things to be moulded, they are people to be unfolded."

~ Jess Lair, author.

1. **Sadness is an inherent part of life**
   We have to accept that sad things are going to happen. But when we understand sadness, and why it's nothing to fear, we can deal with these things calmly and with dignity.

2. **All emotions are valid**
   All our emotions have an equally important role to play and each emotion will serve us well when emotional mastery is in place.

3. **Taking offence is a choice**
   Being offended isn't the automatic reaction we've been raised to believe it is.

4. **An observation isn't a criticism**
   This illustrates how we begin to hear things very differently with an emotional education.

5. **Self, I, and Me all matter**
   It's not possible to pour from an empty cup. Self-care and learning to meet our own needs equals power and self-belief.

6. **Self-aggrandising is vital**
   t's not conceited, 'big-headed 'or egotistical to be aware of your qualities, skills, and achievements.

7. **Disagreement isn't rejection**
   In a disagreement, it's not *you* who's being rejected, it's only your opinion.

8. **Anger isn't abuse**
   It's quite possible to explain your anger without the use of personal insults, threats, hurtful words or recriminations.

9. **Fear isn't the enemy**
   Fear is the body's natural response to a perceived threat. For example, there's no threat when leaving a job you hate to follow your dream of self-employment. The fear comes from the lies you've been told and the misinformation you've been programmed to believe.

10. **Success is not illustrated by wealth**
    While money is important and emotionally educated people are brilliant at making bucketloads of it, true success can't be measured in pounds and pence.

If only we had learned these truths from a young age.

But, instead, we were taught the exact opposite and have learned to live from mind and thinking instead of soul and feeling.

Your mind won't help you

Your mind is a magnificent instrument if you want to perform open heart surgery, compile a shopping list, or complete a word puzzle. But when it comes to all things soulful and emotional, this is not its area of expertise. In fact, it's rubbish at it.

In your most despairing moments, the best your mind will come up with is more of what hasn't worked before in any meaningful and lasting way.

We don't need to feel better, other or different to what we're feeling. And, in fact, there is no better, because there's nothing wrong with what we're already feeling.

Many who embark on a journey of so-called 'healing', reach a point in that journey when it becomes apparent that the root of their suffering is an inability to love themselves. But to truly love ourselves, we must love the Deborah who's sad today or the Johnathon who's scared today — in other words, we must love every aspect of ourselves.

Trying to 'heal' our fear or sadness is to reject ourselves, which isn't self-love or any kind of love.

The freedom to emote without fear

To imagine what we're feeling is a cause for healing — as though it's some type of illness — is to outright reject Self. But for many of us,

Self has been rejected all our lives, by others who couldn't or wouldn't respond to our emotions in a healthy way. And that's been the cause of our pain from the start.

An emotional education gives you the freedom to emote without fear — especially the fear of the reactions and harsh words of other people. And you'll find other people will stop reacting in unwelcome and hurtful ways to the authentic you for one reason, and one reason only — they wouldn't fucking dare!

Emotionally mature people carry an aura of quiet and dignified, yet supreme self-confidence. It shines forth like a beacon of blinding light. It will be evident in your body language, your eyes and your gentle smile. And it will emanate from a compassionate heart that has begun to support those that need it, from a place of pure love, instead of misguided duty.

There may be people in your life who would hurt you for daring to consider your own needs or expressing yourself with emotional honesty. But they're not the type of people who possess the courage to even contemplate upsetting an emotionally intelligent person. They may be a pain in the arse, but they possess that sense of 'knowing', just like you.

Emotional education is your gift to yourself

There's no greater gift you can bestow upon yourself than an emotional education. Because everything that matters so deeply right now becomes trivial, or even funny once that knowledge is in place. And you'll laugh — and most likely facepalm — when you think back to the issues that caused a knot of worry and anxiety in your tummy, but now no longer matter.

Fears fall away without your input or without you having to spend time and money doing a single goddamned thing. Your newly emotionally intelligent self will be given a new pair of spectacles through which to view the world. And you'll begin to see your new world as one with endless possibilities and unlimited potential. Where risk is exciting and what other people think is unimportant.

Knowledge, and knowledge alone, is the key that unlocks the door to **your** ideal treehouse — whatever that looks like for you.

But I'm not talking about the second-best life you strive for here. I'm talking about the first-best life you dream about. The one you tell yourself off for dreaming about in your most private moments, when you allow yourself to dream honestly and let your mind drift off into your soul space. The life you believe is only for other people, like those you compare yourself and your life to.

Your soul doesn't recognise your second-best. It doesn't acknowledge what you're willing to settle for because you are too full of fear and self-doubt to create your first-best. This is because your soul doesn't see you as you see yourself.

You are not your experiences

I never found out who wrote this poem, but I'd love to believe that Soul itself wrote it.

One day, a flawless diamond was thrown into a dirty pond. It lay there on the murky floor for decades, collecting every imaginable bit of sludge, dirt, and shit on top of it.

Then, one day, someone fished it out of the pond and it shone flawlessly in the brilliant sunlight. For all its experiences the diamond never stopped being the embodiment of perfection, beauty, and magnificence — because that was its true nature.

The moral of the poem is, you're not your

experiences, you never were, and you're never going to be.

10.

Freedom and the fully felt feeling

"I tried to drown my sorrows, but the bastards learned how to swim, and now I'm overwhelmed by this decent and good feeling."

~ Frida Kahlo, Mexican painter.

How do we go from a place where we're despairing emotionally to a place where what we're despairing about is perceived as trivial, or even funny. What's the process?

There is no process. There's no ritual or ceremony either. Nor is there anything you need set time aside for in your busy schedule.

Instead, we simply allow ourselves to be present with what we're truly feeling. And we allow ourselves to be acceptable people within that present moment.

Emotion isn't the issue. It never was. What we were raised to believe about the difficult feelings we want to avoid is a big fat lie, born from generational ignorance. The real reason we suffer with unwanted emotions is because we resist them.

Without being aware of it, we first pull in our tummy muscles as a way of lessening the sensation we feel in our solar plexus (the pit of the tummy). This is your soul talking to you, loud and clear. The emotion is seeking your acknowledgement and acceptance.

The second thing we do is allow mind and thinking to take over soul and feeling. We search our database of solutions: therapy, shopping, another healing session, a chat with a friend. And all these things seem to work, but it's only ever temporary.

We rent relief from these issues, but they return repeatedly. The outcome is maxed-out credit cards (great, something else to make life difficult!) and friends who begin to drift away because we keep talking about the same problems — often for years. This adds more loneliness to life when we're already barely coping with a lack of meaningful connection.

But when we allow the emotion to be there, without judgement and without feeling the need to quickly heal it. And when we're not looking for avoidance techniques, talking about it, making it bad or engaging in a distraction, the emotion quickly diminishes. This is something I call 'coming up to move out'.

All words, thoughts, and feelings have an energy signature. Don't worry, I'm not going to go all 'woo-woo' on you here, but I will give you an example.

Somebody unexpectedly, but deliberately, says, 'BOO!' to you to scare you. When you jump slightly or move your upper body backwards, your body is responding to the energy between you and the person that tried to scare you. Your first instinct is to put distance between you and this person — and that emotion is felt in the chest.

This emotion remains stored in your physical body until the person reassures you, they were only joking and apologises for having a laugh at your expense. But when you were growing up, that never happened.

Everything changes when we learn to accept the apology we never got.

Right now, your body is fit to bursting with the unresolved emotion. This emotion comes from every event in your life when you were not allowed to express what you were feeling. Nobody explained. Nobody apologised. Nobody helped you make sense of why your emotions were belittled, trivialised or disregarded. Or why you had to be chastised for them.

When we feel sadness, we can be quick to label it as depression. But it's simply your soul saying, 'Hi, I'm a little bit of the sadness you are storing. I can't hurt you, but if you acknowledge me, accept me and don 'loathe me, then I'll go away."

It does indeed then go away — and much faster than you might imagine. The space it leaves behind is then filled with feelings of self-confidence, self-love, and fearlessness.

This goes on and on, with every emotion you stop resisting, stop demonising and stop attempting to avoid.

This is because you're saying, loud and clear, "I am acceptable with this emotion." In other words, you're loving yourself, regardless of how you're feeling. I'll share a story with you about my own experiences.

When I finally stopped New-Aging (renting temporary relief from the emotions I'd labelled as 'depression'), I felt those emotions were going to eat me alive.

I didn't have a plan. I wasn't sat there, wondering what would happen if I stopped healing. I didn't even consider if anything would happen!

But I was determined to survive — and equally determined to stay away from my doctor and his happy pills. This meant I was left with no choice but to feel whatever I was feeling.

It took a while for me to connect the dots. For the first six months I hadn't been aware that every time I gave in to what I was feeling, I felt more confident, less scared, and had a lot more energy. But when the penny finally dropped, I began to understand that these new feelings of peace, and absence of mind chatter, were because I was acknowledging my emotions instead of trying to 'heal 'them.

Once I cracked it, I was living fearlessly and had stopped giving a single flying fuck about what anyone thought of me. Then, one morning, I experienced the most extraordinary thing...

I woke up with what felt like a huge black

cloud hanging over my head. It felt so real it was as though I could reach out and touch it. The cloud was accompanied by a deep, deep sorrow, so my first instinct was to roll over, get comfy and stay in bed. But then, I felt a sense of absolute joy!

Now, if you had a challenging childhood, with less than capable parents, you'll know it's not unusual for us to image that we are losing the plot from time to time. And this moment, for me, was one of them. I was in shock and disbelief, because I was acutely aware that I was feeling sorrow from the depths of hell — and joy — simultaneously!

I wondered, how could this be? And Soul replied, "The sorrow is just there."

It was a turning point in my recovery. In fact, it was the biggest turning point. I began to understand that I was, in fact, joyous that morning and looking forward to the day ahead — but an old sorrow had come up to be acknowledged.

I felt it so fully, tears appeared — but I went about my business, allowing its presence and knowing it couldn't hurt me. The sorrow dissipated throughout the day, but the joy never left me.

The next thing I knew, I was experiencing levels of personal empowerment, fearlessness, self-love and confidence I never imagined I'd be able to attain.

We need to be willing to learn about and understand our uncomfortable emotions. Because when we stop thinking of them as something bad and stop resisting them, they'll simply 'come up to move out'.

It's simple and, above all, painless. With your new-found knowledge and skills, those uncomfortable emotions will simply 'be there 'and the pay-off, when you no longer resist them, is the life you've always dreamed about.

The Guest House, by Rumi

This being human is a guest house.
Every morning a new arrival.

A joy, a depression, a meanness,
some momentary awareness comes
as an unexpected visitor.

Welcome and entertain them all!
Even if they're a crowd of sorrows,
who violently sweep your house
empty of its furniture,
still, treat each guest honourably.
He may be clearing you out
for some new delight.

The dark thought, the shame, the malice,
meet them at the door laughing,
and invite them in.

Be grateful for whoever comes,
because each has been sent
as a guide from beyond.

11.

Introducing The Panacea Program

If you've found this book helpful and would like to take your emotional education to the next level, I invite you to join me on The Panacea Program.

The Program is a learning experience that will teach you how to recognise and handle your emotions in everyday life.

I chose the name 'Panacea 'because a panacea is a 'cure all' and emotional literacy is a solution to most problems.

But the Program is not just for whatever is going on in your life right now—it's a resource for life. It will help you continue reaching your potential and living your life to the fullest for as long as you live.

When you begin to learn about your own emotions and those of others, you and your life will change quickly and in the most remarkable ways.

Your worth will no longer depend on anything or anybody else. You'll begin to develop the composure, discernment, and emotional maturity you need to stand in your own power and be unapologetically authentic.

The Panacea Program creates a joyous ripple effect. It's not just you who'll get to live a conflict-free, empowered life. What you learn will positively impact your family, friends, work colleagues and the wider world — because the world needs emotional education more than it needs anything else.

Your path to emotional freedom and the life you've always wanted starts here:

www.theacademyofemotionaleducation.com

Afterword

"People don't grow up, they get married, have children, find parking spaces, and honour their credit cards, this isn't maturing, this is ageing"

~Maya Angelou

If we want the happiness and fulfilment our hearts long for, we sometimes have to look at what we would prefer not to see.

The characteristics of an emotionally mature individual include a willingness to:

- Be comfortable with criticism
- Accept responsibility for the part we play in the creation of our own pain and conflicts — both inner and outer
- Attempt to understand, instead of punishing and apportion blame
- Not give a care in the world about what others think

- Stand resolutely in your own power, taking ownership of your destiny, opinions, and the way you choose to live your life
- Welcome risk and be unafraid of failure.

But the ultimate definition is when someone hurts us, even when it's painful and deliberate, we attempt to understand them. And, if possible, we help them instead of hurting them back.

Ninety eight percent of us never stood a chance of achieving emotional maturity. We were set up to fail from the moment we were born. As our parents, or primary caregivers, programmed us to fear our natural emotions. And we learned to compartmentalise them, to the point where, in adulthood, we go to the most extraordinary lengths to avoid them. At the cost of our happiness, health, and often even our sanity.

The emotions we were taught to deny, disguise, and distort — then, later, 'heal' — are no more a threat to us than a week-old kitten. Yet our fear of them is entrenched.

Rather than allowing ourselves to feel these

emotions, we avoid them. And we cling to what's familiar — even when it's toxic — because, to us, that feels safer.

The depth of pain we feel every day makes us desperate for change. But we fear change as much as we crave it, because it might incur the anger and disapproval of others.

But are these others worth your sacrifice?

Their anger comes from their own pain, under-achieving or disillusionment with life. You can't help them any more than they can help you. And, in the meantime, all you're doing is keeping each other trapped in a cycle of misery.

You might find solace in shopping, therapy, alcohol or the vain hope that one day things will get better. But all this is doing is numbing the pain.

Sadly, without meaningful change, things are unlikely to get better. You may never experience love in the soulful sense of the word or have the supportive friends you deserve. And you may never feel properly understood, listened to or validated.

Honest introspection is hard when we're already in the depths of self-loathing. The last thing we want to do is listen to anything that would add to the endless self-criticism: an inner dialogue that plays on a loop, especially at bedtime.

But for many of us our destiny in life is to break the cycle. To achieve what we previously considered impossible and to live the kind of life that we currently only imagine.

To get there we must first be willing to accept that we do play a part in our own suffering. This is something rarely touched on in the world of self-help, therapy, or New-Age healing. They'll sugar-coat it for us, then follow it with sympathy, empathy, and soothing noises. But this isn't what we need.

What we really need is a reality check: to be challenged and to be open to the emotional education we never received in childhood.

And I know you can handle it, because your job is to do my job, and teach of love.

Printed in Great Britain
by Amazon